PASSION
Fruits

By: Lauren "Lush" Collier

Written and Illustrated
By
Lauren "Lush" Collier

Contents

Contents

In Loving Memory

Maya Angelou born Marguerite Annie Johnson; April 4, 1928 – May 28, 2014) was an American author, poet, dancer, actress and singer. Throughout the years she received dozens of awards and more than 50 honorary degrees. She was an actor, writer, director, and producer of plays, movies, and public television programs. She was active in the Civil Rights movement, and worked with Martin Luther King, Jr. and Malcolm X. She was respected as a spokesperson for black people and women, and her extraordinary works have been considered a defense of Black culture worldwide. Maya Angelou is a true Legend and Icon and will forever be appreciated and missed.

"Phenomenal Woman"
By: Maya Angelou

Pretty women wonder where my secret lies.
I'm not cute or built to suit a fashion model's
size
But when I start to tell them,
They think I'm telling lies.
I say,
It's in the reach of my arms
The span of my hips,
The stride of my step,
The curl of my lips.
I'm a woman
Phenomenally.
Phenomenal woman,
That's me.

I walk into a room
Just as cool as you please,

(Continued...)

And to a man,
The fellows stand or
Fall down on their knees.
Then they swarm around me,
A hive of honey bees.
I say,
It's the fire in my eyes,
And the flash of my teeth,
The swing in my waist,
And the joy in my feet.
I'm a woman
Phenomenally.
Phenomenal woman,
That's me.

Men themselves have wondered
What they see in me.
They try so much
But they can't touch
My inner mystery.
When I try to show them
They say they still can't see.

(Continued...)

I say,
It's in the arch of my back,
The sun of my smile,
The ride of my breasts,
The grace of my style.
I'm a woman

Phenomenally.
Phenomenal woman,
That's me.

Now you understand
Just why my head's not bowed.
I don't shout or jump about
Or have to talk real loud.
When you see me passing
It ought to make you proud.
I say,
It's in the click of my heels,
The bend of my hair,
the palm of my hand,
The need of my care,

(Continued...)

'Cause I'm a woman
Phenomenally.
Phenomenal woman,
That's me.

DEDICATION & THANKS

To my mother Lynette, thank you for remaining strong throughout the trying years, and for holding the family together after daddy's passing in 2010. Mom, with much gratitude thank you for all you do. To my father Joe, you remain the inspiration for my writings and give me strength and aspiration to follow my dreams! To my brother Joseph, you make me a very proud little sister and I know you will continue to make our family proud. I Love You Mom, Dad, and Joseph.

To my family, fans and supporters, thank you for believing in me and please continue to accompany me on this wondrous journey. I Love and appreciate you all!

Also if you haven't done so already, check out my first book "Sundae Poetry" and a great book that I edited and illustrated "Thoughts of a Kinetic Mind" by Prince Isaac. Available on Amazon, Createspace, Barnes and Nobles online and etc...

Lush
"Three Shots Max"

Real lovers are like a tight pair of jeans, hard to
slip in
Not even the prettiest person could come
between them
You and I against the world, that's what it used to
feel like
Lately, everything you've been doing ain't
nowhere near right
We feel like strangers, we ain't nowhere near
tight
I swear I'm so far ahead, you can only see my rear
lights
Thought I had enough armor around my heart,
guess I wasn't geared right.

Bang, bang, bang! When you gonna stop shooting
me down to the ground?
And you ask why I sport a frown...
Because you chase every ass and skirt that pops in
town
and you don't care if they're 'pops' in your town,
nor if their 'pops is around
Red bones or pretty brown browns

Think it's my time to send back a couple of them
rounds
I been a Queen, you just never gave me the crown
I don't need it no way, so don't try to give it to me
now.

I know it's nice of me to give a three shots max
You've reached the top; tell me how was the
climax?
Strings cut, there ain't no way to climb back
Stabbed in the back, no dagger, no ax
How you doing? When can I see you? Questions
you better not ask
Facts, I had to give dude the ax
It wasn't easy but nothing really is
Love don't live here anymore, I often wonder if it
ever did.

Lush
"Heart Strong"

My backbone? I misplaced that
months back when you took control over
my mind, body and soul
Fighting to get it back
Sometimes I'd give up, especially when you'd
make those puppy dog eyes
Baby this, baby that, running your fingertips up
my thighs, remember that?
Those days came, now they're gone
A woman scorn makes a heart strong
Despite being a few times torn
In due time, the pieces again combine
What was yours was never mine
But I gave you everything, never mind
I tell it every time, nothing changes
I never even nagged or ranted
You wanted it? Wishes I granted
Ungrateful! That was you
Fed you love with such a hearty spoonful
and all I got was some stale crumbs
They say have your fun while you're still young,
and together I thought we did that

This is where home's at
Here lays your fabrics, aroma and all of your fitted
caps, but I guess that didn't matter
Wish you didn't take up so much space in my
heart...Matter.

Lush
"Keep your lies"

Out the mouth flew lies automatically
Don't bother me, shoo fly! Screaming all
dramatically
Ducking, dodging for what was sad to see
Lies that came in a swarm
I wonder if liars were made or even possibly born
"I lie because I love you"
Save that cliché for a person that was born only
yesterday
If you truly care
Half the shit you do, you wouldn't dare
Who you fooling dear?
No spooning here
You blew that, when she blew you
Got the bad news, yea a little crucial
Now I do me, so continue to do you…

From a distance you can smell the bliss
Crazy how I can't even reminisce, 'cause with you
I never felt like this
It's a brand new feeling
Feeling so rich like my money's to the ceiling
In the book, you've called me every bitch,

like I have no feelings
It's your time to rot, cavities...no filling
Hope that other chick still finds you appealing
when all the fake and phony out of your pores,
start spilling
Guts you start spilling
But I could care less, it's far too late
Should have never jumped ship in a shallow ass
lake
Should have never took the bait
Should have never eaten the crumbs off another
woman's plate
Keep your lies
Man I'm straight!

Lush
"Magic"

   Up and down he swore,
to not allow his battered heart to love once
more...
Tougher than spikes on a leather jacket
He was harder than hard core...
But here comes the magic
Someone that he said time after time wasn't his
type
Someone he made jokes of, all day and all night...
The same person he rarely hugged, rubbed and
kissed
Became the one person when lonesome he
dangerously missed.

   Hurtful words seemed to always escape his
mouth
When all she ever wanted for him was a promising
route...
All he did was doubt what together the two could
amount
With all the good she'd done, only the bad he kept
count...

His favorite motto, "I need a bad bitch"
But this type of bad bitch came in a different
form, a different package
Her head strong, cold hands, heart warm...
Physical fuller than what his eyes and hands
desired
She was so "bad" that she was good for him,
someone his mother aspired.

   He's not a magical lover boy
Just a dash of sensitivity
Not a wealthy man
Just a handful of consistency
Not the most affectionate
Just a lot of quality time and persistency
Not the most mature guy
But Just about the right one for me.

Lush
"What Lies Beneath"

Was it ever really there?
Or did it only exist in my head
What my eyes saw, an eye sore
Surely didn't expect this to be in store.

Must have left and came back about ten times
Ten times too many
Hurt, disappointments? I've felt plenty
Sympathy and pity
Gave everything, love, hate, quality time
and plenty of pennies.

Never felt this betrayed
One, I became your slave
Two, I believed your lies
Three, I put up with the bull
Four, I loved you so
What once was is now no mo'!

I think this is the part where I'm supposed to get
mad! Get even!
I win by walking away
Leaving you in the dust
Give you kind words to remember me by
for in the end, what's the sense of you seeing me
cry?
When in the past, to all your boys, you just
laughed
No matter the tears, and how hard I sighed and
huffed
"She'll be back!" you'd say with a chest so puffed.

It's time that "we"
No longer be a we
No longer be a team
No... longer... be
It's time that I get to know I, myself and me
As good as it will be
'Cause no one will ever, treat me as good, as me.

Lush
"Different Page"

I gave it all, what's left?
When I went right, you went left
When I looked back you looked forward
When you were holding back I was so forward
On a different page that's what I called it
Over looked all the fouls you made when I should
have called it
If I made a booboo
Constantly you'd nag and boohoo
I did everything a man was "supposed" to do
So from a distance you couldn't tell who's who
Now I'm sure that had to hurt
But all I ever did was hurt
And unlike you
I'm never spiteful, plus ungrateful?
What a dangerous duo
Trio, if I add the liar in you
I can't forget the thief acts
You can't be mad; I'm just speaking the facts
Many, many tears just follow the tracks
Many, mini tears I should have known
it was all an act.

We're on a different page
So when I turn to the next chapter
There's no going back after
Nope! And I don't need to re-read for I didn't miss a thing
Damn! You're sure gonna miss this thang'!

Lush
"So Long my Love, So Long"

The night slowly crept upon us
We laughed and joked the entire day
but when darkness arises I turn into someone else
I wore a puffed chest and a flared nose
Foul words endlessly flew out of my mouth
I was a beast! I was your beast, but for how long?

You'd always threaten that my outbursts would
drive you away
Never did I think that the day would be today
You packed up your bags and you threw me
your key...
My lips you kissed ever so gently
I didn't want our lips to ever part
You took up the entire space in my heart
But my temper I couldn't control

The alley was dark, and I begged you to stay
The rain fogged up your Prada glasses
You wore the rain coat I bought you last Christmas
In fact we had matching coats

You were my match...
The calm to my storm
You were the reason I began to love again
All the joy we shared flashed before my eyes
My heart wouldn't stop palpitating
I yelled at the top of my lungs
"I Love You! I love you! Please don't leave me!"
You looked in my direction and blew your last kiss
My eyes filled with heavy tears
I then knew I had lost you forever
The biggest part of my heart, ripped out!
So long my Love, so long.

Lush
"Not the Only One"

So tonight makes the third night in the row that
you arrive home late
and again you say "baby I had a long night at the
office, I promise to make it up to you."
You can keep that story Charles, I don't want it

This perfectly prepared dinner is now ice cold
And this once perfectly whole heart is now too
Oh I saw those lipstick stains on your collar last
night
and I can smell her cheap perfume on you right
now!
"Honey I-"
Honey nothing! There is nothing sweet in this
damn house anymore.
2 months and 3 days, that's how long I've
projected this affair has been going on
I haven't said one word, I've just been gathering
all the essentials.
The Marriot on Broadway, on Fridays
Her apartment in Soho, on Tuesdays
All of the fine dining, the gifts
Oh boy those gifts, those matching gifts,

the same that you try to buy me with
But I can never be bought!
My loyalty and love should have amounted to the
sky
But like an old toy you pushed me to the side
Took me for granted
You thought I'd remain by your side?
Is that how dumb and gullible you portray me as?
Oh now when I'm asking you questions you have
no tongue?!
"Doll, you are so right, I am utterly apologetic, I
lost my head for a minute, but, but just know she
means nothing to me, and it is you and has always
been you."

That was...typical
You cheated and got caught
If I never caught you, you'd still be fucking her
Still be kissing another woman's lips
Gripping another woman's hips
And for that your bags are already packed
You can send for your other things later
"Baby please don't-!"
*'Cause when you call me baby, I know I'm not the
only one...*

Lush
"A Blessing and a Curse"

Wow! You know girl, for someone who's been
through a lot
you seem to always be smiling
But, but you've been burned so many times, yet I
barely see the wounds
you must be quite good at hiding them, "yup
that's what most assume"
Sweeping them in a tight corner, you must have a
magical broom?
(With a smile I say) "It's not that I conceal them
but with time helps heal them."

I often do wonder if the ones that have hurt me
are hurting others, or perhaps helping them.
I'm hoping that they've learned from their prior
mistakes and that this would lead to no more
heart breaks
Sometimes; usually when I'm alone, I can still feel
my heart ache
But I know that turning bitter would only make it
worse.

I tell myself that this great heart of mine,
this big clump of sunshine, is really a blessing and
a curse.

Naïve I tend to be, wishing that I wasn't
Okay! No problem! Yes! Of course! Sure! Why
Not! Anytime!

Now this one needs that, that one needs this
I'm really getting overwhelmed from all of the
bullshit
Can't remember the last time I was that needy
A child I must have been
Leeching from my parents' pot of gold
"Stay in a child's place" I was told
The right to need my parents is one of the perks
That was then, now I'm grown.
We're grown and the only need we should need is
their love
If fed with the right nourishment to succeed in
this unpredictable world,
then fine is what we shall hopefully be
Bliss is what we would find after seeking
No palm readers, hey! No peeking.

This big clump of sunshine can really be a
rainstorm...
After all the aiding and assisting who is left to give
me a hand?
A shoulder, a pat on the back or even some
quarters to make a call?
A lift from the mall?
Glass slippers for a ball?
Anything at all?

Lush
"All of These Damn Tears"

Ever given so much, just to receive so little?
Ever lost it all and needed a helping hand to once
again stand? But for some reason it was never
extended
I guess having someone's back went out of
season.
Love shouldn't be full of lies and deceit
Constantly thinking of ways to use and misuse
So constantly I'm throwing missiles and running
out of tissue
Soaking wet but I keep on blowing
Never seen these eyes so puffy, so swollen
Nah I ain't get hit in the face, but I've been dished
some blows
Lows and highs, and I wear a disguise but still
somehow everyone knows.

I'd close my eyes but they wouldn't stay shut
I got work in the morning and can't afford to call
in, but I'm going insane,
there's just too much of you on the membrane!

Can't move, heart's heavy, knees feeling all weak.
Then we go through a silent phase, won't text,
and won't speak
Shoot, that's when I'm thinking of you the most
And though you hurt me continuously, I still want
you close, silly of me!
Damn these feelings, and these everlasting tears
of mine.

I'm a pushover if I don't speak my mind
When I start complaining I have too much of a
spine?
I just can't win
Pool full of problems and I definitely can't swim
Being as literal as I can be
Frank, blunt and all the way down to the Tee
But I'm always gonna be all the way me!
Never been fake, and especially never been a
snake
Don't let the hissing fool you
Take a seat and let some REAL MEN school you!

I'll admit that I too, could stand to take a class or
two
Yes, even I still have a lot to learn
Searching for happiness, wondering when it shall
be my turn?
I hear that it starts within,
so I shouldn't have to travel far
Never bitter, I still keep my heart ajar.
Now I make sure I do my research before
I approve the final draft
Hats off to the everlasting couples, I'm so hoping
to capture the love you have.

Lush
"Unseen"

I saw you when you followed her
Her beauty drew you in
I wished it was me instead
But instead it only occurred in a picture I drew you
in

I saw the smile she flashed as you gave her a
compliment
Her sex appeal you praised
I wished it was me instead
But wishful thinking was a no no' in the household
I was raised

She saw me when I walked by
But her presence left you blind
You didn't look in my direction
Maybe distracted by her body's reflection
In my head I contemplated an intersection
But myself I had to question
How more alive did I have to be, for you to
acknowledge me?
Don't give me your pity; I'm not looking for an
apology

Today I say no more!
No more trying to be seen
So unseen I remain.

Lush
"Ride or Die"

I don't really want to question you
Don't want do what the rest would do
And I don't beg, no I don't plead
But I thought you knew me, thought I knew you...
We were super cool since preschool
Wore the same jays, shared the same toys
What happened to that boy?
You held me down when everyone else was afraid
to...
Played house in the park and we both said I do,
and I really did...
So what really did transpire?
Was it enough to make this friendship expire?
With the writing and rapping, u really inspired me
to keep going...
When the rest said, "girl u ain't blowing"
Up! Is where we were heading
I felt it in my blood, you was my blood but I didn't
even notice it shedding
Damn, I wish that I could turn back the hands
of time so we could make it all better, however,
I know it can't be...

They say to keep it moving like leaves on a tree
But you were such a big part of me...
Shit you was damn near the heart of me
Hard for me to see a better day
without you by my side bebe'
Wish we were still kids, bebe'
No drama, when all we did was laugh and play

When people changed up on you like u was new in
town, who was really down when things went
down?
Looked around there was no one to be found
Not a soul huh? Just I
You taught me if it don't apply let it fly
'Cause only you knew how I got sometimes
You know I could get real cold like Pluto
Stretch a chick's face like Pinocchio's nose
Hard to tell your friends from your foes
But we got really good at it
This music we got really good at it
Became a microphone addict
You was the bomb too, kaboom!
Even built a studio in the attic
Together we were a classic.

Lush
 "For Years Forever"

For years I've been looking for someone to love
me like you did...
Four years

For years I've been empty, looking for a fulfillment
Four years

For years I've been alone, wishing I were able to
pick up a phone and just call you...
Four years

For years I've been lost, lost without your
guidance and knowledge...
Four years

For years I've cried tears, some of happiness, but
most were of pain...
Four years

It's been four long years...

For years you were my best friend...
Forever

For years you were my hero...
Forever

For years you were my rock...
Forever

For years you taught me, held me and protected
me...
Forever

For years you loved me, and I will always love you
Forever

It will be forever, it will always be forever, you will
always be forever...
In my heart, in my soul, in my mind...in me.

Lush
"A Father's Love"

No love is like a parent's love
They will love you whether you're right or wrong
Hug and kiss you when at your smelliest
And give it to you straight when you start to screw up!

No love is like a mother's love
Worrying when you're perfectly fine
Patching up your boo-boos even when you can do it yourself
And prying into your business, which can be a good and bad thing (Trust me!)

No love is like a father's love this I surely know
Tough but kind, smart and goofy, brave and sometimes timid
High fives and horse playing, bike riding lessons and plenty of sports
Quality time and get out of my face time
Don't tell mom, here's a few bucks time
I might not always be home, but I'm always on time, time.

Father, dad, daddy, pops, old man, pop dukes whichever you prefer.
The love you guys give is so much needed and appreciated
Though you may not be around as much as you'd like
In our hearts we know you're there
Maybe not in the stadium, but you're cheering us on
Maybe not at a school play, but you're applauding hard
Some of us never met our dads; some of us have and wish we hadn't
Some of us have just sperm donors or at least that's what it seems
Some of us have our dad's at home with us
And some of us had our dads for a short period of time
But in that time the love was so strong that it still feels like we have them for eternity.

Lush
"He Lives On"

It's in everything I do
It's in everything I say
It's in the way I move, and sometimes in the way I
groove
The way I sing and the way I yell
Everyday it's in effect and it's not hard to tell

It's in the way I cry and as usual you're the reason
why
It's in the way I sigh and usually you're the reason
why

It's in the way I love
It's in the way I dislike
It's in my views and opinions, and in my duties
and commitments
The way I smile and the way I frown
Everyday it's in effect and it'll never die down

It's in the way I laugh and as usual you're the
reason why

It's in the way I smirk and usually you're the
reason why

You're living vicariously through me and everyday
it shows
Gone too soon, but only God knows
Some people are never shown what a hero is
Some people have different meanings
It could be their dog, mother, father, kids,
sister, brother, neighbor,
teacher, preacher, or motivational speaker.

The tears are boundless, I can't stop em'
no matter how hard I try
A love song, a sing along, a duet
Sipping on Jack or some Moet, nice and wet
The China Buffet or a nice lil matinee'
EVERYTHING, every single thing, I keep you with
me
My shadow, my guard, my guardian angel
I Thank You.

Lush
"Hidden Agenda"

    He was caught by surprise by the beaming sun
It brought out his eyes, the beaming sun
He was told stories by his mom about girls like me
It brought out his curiosity, about girls like me

    I would provoke him with my risen dress by the
shore of the ocean
It grew and widened his wandering eyes, by the
shore of the ocean
He was told stories by his older sister about girls
like me
It brought out his curiosity, about girls like me

    See now I was oblivious that I held such a
reputation
But I wanted to make sure that I didn't let
"Mr. Curiosity" down
The bait was placed and boy did he bite
I thought he would have been eaten up by my
body's influential waves
But he swam with the tide
He unleashed the beast he was attempting to hide

She was caught by surprise by the beaming sun
It brought out her smile, the beaming sun
I told my daughter stories about boys like him
They might look like they'll drown,
but baby! Can they swim!

Lush
"Timmy's Eyes"

His eyes told stories of his past...
How humble he became
How strong and confident he was

Love frightened him and it showed in his eyes
What a flirtatious beast he was
and he was extremely single to my surprise

Deep was an understatement for the description
of his eyes, they were simply beautiful, **genuine**
As if he could see through me, right to the core
His stare let off so much heat; it was the fire in his
eyes

In his eyes, I could get lost
In Timmy's eyes
I wondered what he saw when he looked at me
with eyes so pure
I wondered if he saw anything at all

In Timmy's Eyes.

Lush
"Blinded"

Waving hips and lusty eyes
She wore...
Striking lips and husky thighs
She wore...

Shallow and bitter
She was...
Mischievous and deceitful
She was...and you knew that

But you still wanted her
You still overlooked the sweetheart from Alabama
The girl who brought you homemade muffins to
work every week
The one who blushed at your touch

Pretty long dresses and long bouncy curls
She wore...
Enchanting smile and soft cream pearls
She wore...

Wise and kind
She was...

Genuine and honest
She was...and you knew that

But you still chose the girl who would break your
heart into a thousand pieces
The one who would stare into your eyes and tell
your ears what they wanted to hear
You knew she was no good for you but you just
had to have her

Ms. Sweetheart took away the homemade
assorted muffins
And the intellectual conversations grew shorter
and shorter
You were no longer the reason behind her bright
smile

Ms. Bad girl grew bored with you
So like her old toys she got rid of you
Your heart was dismantled
And you were looking for some consoling
But no one was around
That sweet girl that would have normally been
there, was tired of being unnoticed
She had finally found someone to appreciate her

You were sad and alone
And that year was the year you learned a valuable
lesson

To value those who value you
To evaluate people in your life thoroughly
And to never bite the hand that feeds you.

Lush
"Me Oh My"

Appreciated by few, affiliated with many
To be funny they called me mini...mouse?
No I'm not that quiet
Never been skinny, food tastes great when you fry
it, you should try it
If unhappy I cause a riot, middle finger I fly it,
no pilot
But I've changed since then, not so much my
physique I'm still far from thin
Beauty on the out, overflowing from within
I was taught to love the skin that I'm in
But there are always improvements, please do it
for yourself, and not the satisfactory of anyone
else.

I've read it, I wrote it, If I like something I quote it
Sometimes timorous, but usually I'm pretty heroic
I'm pretty? I know it (hush, you're making me
blush)
Independent woman and I proudly show it
Not a bragger or a boaster
Real as they come, no poser
Picture perfect, yes I'm a poser

Poetry composer
A temper, but I try to keep my composure
Make boo-boos? Yes, I may ask if I can start over
Or I might just continue, I bet it still sounds good
Sometimes I don't make sense, I just babble
I'm guilty, but no need to pick up the gavel
Spontaneous, I just might pick up and travel,
to a faraway place, with different sand and gravel.

Happy to be alive, in the past I didn't care
Selfish I was, my dad had to constantly remind me
He said think of the ones that love you,
do you think that parents should bury their child?
Had to snap out of that type of thinking
Young, dumb, what was I thinking?
Rushing to get old, though they warned me to
slow down
You know me, stubborn to the bone
Queen of this throne, but it was my momma's
home
So who am I kidding?
Stepped into the real world
Wish I could take a step back, but this is life
So life, HERE I AM!

Lush
"Confidence"

In my shoes, they'd never been
In my pool, they'll never swim
Full-figured, never been thin
So they figured I'd never fit in

"You're pretty for a big girl"
Why can't I be just pretty...period?
But as I aged I got over that period
My persona alone leaves minds blown
So gifted and talented, yes I should be cloned
That way when I climb upon the throne
I wouldn't have to hold it down all on my own

Shoulders still upright,
though I carry the world...
Bitter people enter my life,
yet I'm still the sweetest girl
Except when I'm pushed to that point
And all people could do is stare
and not dare to point
I tear it up when it needs to be torn
Not the easiest life, but this girl will never be
scorned.

Lush
"Why I write"

For eyes that cannot see or weep
Hands that cannot write
Words that you cannot find
To express what is on your mind
You shall have no worries
For this is why I write...

When my dad said *"You have such a way with
words, how you put them together so beautifully"*
When my friends listen with their eyes
And respond with their smiles and smirks
When my words bring out emotions that one
never knew they had
Yes, this is why I write...

For the shy and afraid
Strong and brave, weird and regular
Saints and misbehaves
For everyone that ever needed a poem to recite
Oh yes! This is why I write.

For the hard heads and soft hearts
Young and the old
Smooth criminals and butter fingered screw-ups
The know it all's and know it not's
The tough as nails and stomach's filled with knots
When the sun is its shiniest and the rain seems to
not want to stop
Yup, that's right, this is why I write!

Lush
"High sky"

Hi sky! High sky!
My limit you are
A little timid some are
but I'm not one of them, by far
My ex told me I was living a fairy tale,
a once upon a time...
That I was dumb, delusional and simply out of my
mind
A simple minded kind of guy
With such a lack of guide
Not enough support and way too much pride.
But I know my limit!
How much I can take, when enough is really
enough
How far I can go, and just how to get there
Hard work does pay off, so don't tell me it doesn't
Was there through it all, so don't tell me I wasn't.

Hi sky! High sky!
My limit you are
A little timid some are
But I'm not one of them, by far.

I may procrastinate a bit
Get discouraged and throw a hissy fit
Sometimes I'm lazy and foolish
Sometimes my temper explodes and I lose it.
Quickly I'd get back on track, because I've got so
much to do, so much to accomplish
I know some people that don't set goals,
that don't have a plan
That, I just don't understand.
Now I know I wake up and go with the flow
But I know my flow is heading in the right
direction.
Life throws blows, puts up obstacles and
intersections
But you must find a method to the madness,
and get pass this!
Know your limit, the high sky!

Lush
"Recognition"

I laid the foundation for those who had their
hands out
Everything was planned out
Thought I'd be re-paid with no doubt in my mind
But friendships and relationships had me so blind
Robbed me blind
Felt like I had a knife to my spine
Pity, kindness and a gullible state of mind should
never be combined
I figured my size and this temper of mine,
would make them show recognition
No pot to piss in, but they keep pissing anyway
And when I say no, I swear they feel some type of
way
Like I owe them something,
when I owe them nothing!
Like it's my duty to give em' the goods when they
ask *"can I hold a lil something."*
I used to have it, now I don't
and I don't even say *"oh I wish I could"*
'Cause that would be me frontin'
and I don't do any of that

With all the good I do, I don't even get a pat on
the back
A cookie, a biscuit, a lil snacky snack
Zero, nil, nada
I give my blood, sweat, tears and the whole
freakin' enchilada.
I'm venting for a reason
A cause, what I believe in
Give credit where credit's due
Don't bite the hand that feeds you
Love who loves you
and when it's all said and done
It's just me, myself and I
No bullets, no gun
I ain't going out like that!
I never get too stressed
For I am way too blessed
After the boycott and protest
I go home to pray and rest
and for those who've done me wrong,
I still wish them the best
For I'm still standing strong
and I know for sure that this was just a test all
along.

Lush
"Divergence"

Eyes to the front but I never see it coming
Eyes glued at my face but they aint saying nothing
Wondering what's she gonna do next
Wondering if he's soon to be my ex
Hoping and praying for my failure and downfall
Hoping that I won't get back up, and just lose it all
What a shame it is, we were so close as kids
What a shame it is, the same place we once lived
The difference is, all you do is take and I truly give
The difference is, you breathe and I really live
When I say it, I really do it
When I say it, I show the proof to prove it
Can't stop me, if they're in my way I tell em'
move it!
Can't stop me, my temper gets lost; really don't
make me lose it!
Pretty sight to see, nope not when I'm a beast
Pretty sight to see, yup to say the least
Bet your bottom dollar, I get the job done
Bet your bottom dollar, your time will come.

Lush
"Hands Up"

Hands up, this is a sign of surrendering
but they still shoot anyway
Hands where I can see them!
but for what? They still shoot anyway
Try to walk away, and guns they spray
A bullet enters from the back
Now it's a war, we're under attack
Eyes bloody it's getting hard to see,
hard to breathe, but I'm still here
Now they want to put a charge on me
The nerve of these people
All eyes on me
And they say we are free?
Free from what?
I'm still trying to find out
Moved out the hood, but we still need a way out
No matter where we go, racism still exists
Our hands are up
But to shoot us...they still insist
Might as well assist
Put the gun in our hand and watch us take the
shot...bloah! Happy now?

Lush
"Idolized"

Fantasized by the size of her thighs
Idolized for the measurement of her waistline
So she stays in the gym to keep trim
She bends and she stretches
She stretches and she bends

Many men yell
"Can I get in? Damn ma how can I get in!"

Fantasized by the size of her thighs
Idolized for the measurement of her waistline
So she stays in the gym to keep trim
She bends and she stretches
She stretches and she bends

Many men yell
"Can I get in? Damn ma how can I get in!"
So he stays at the gym to keep buff and trim
He bends and he stretches
He stretches and he bends
He plays the gym with all of his men
But they ain't really his friends
He's just using them to ride shot gun to their Benz

Forty years old living with his momma
And no he don't pay rent
He don't lift a hand
And He damn sure ain't got a j.o.b

Fantasized by the size of her thighs
Idolized for the measurement of her waistline
So she stays in the gym to keep trim
She bends and she stretches
She stretches and she bends

Every day he watches her, fantasying
 "Damn baby I just wanna get in, how can I get in?"

Finally she says "Answer me this, how you trynna get in, when you can't even get in your own car?
Your own house, your own business?
Man get a job, and do something with your life
There's plenty of resources
What you too ashamed to stand on the unemployment line?
Yeah you might look fine and your body's all gorgeous, but what's a nice body without a brain?
Now idolize that.

Lush
"Free-spirited"

Blend in?
Follow the crowd?
Well I'm too different to blend in
And that crowd, I just don't know where they're
headed
But I know we're I came from
And from there, only up is where I'll go

Different perspective?
Why can't I just follow the trends?
We'll I'm too free-spirited to be categorized, to be
placed in a box
And that trend, will be old news next week
And I'm here to stay, to forever be remembered

I will speak up when others can't
Use my pen when others want to use a sword
For the pen will always be much mightier
I will stand firm on my beliefs
even when I am the only one standing
when others are too afraid and need a voice
let me be your choice
I will not hide

Fight?
Follow my instinct?
You damn right I'll fight
Fight for what's right even when they say I'm
wrong
I'll follow what my gut says
But also take it up with my mind and my heart
'Cause I'm still human

Yes, I am human
Graceful, resilient and free
Free to speak, free to write, free to stand
I won't fall in line, life is not a straight path, nor is
it meant to be
I won't follow the crowd for I know not where
they go
I won't be just a trend
I want my name to be long-lived
And my actions to speak louder than my words
I will be Great!

Lush
"I can't be Without You"

The sunset turns the sky a reddish hue
Still I can't be without you

The sun's rays turn the rain into a magical rainbow
But still I can't be without you

All so beautiful, so pure and so distinct
But without you my feelings are extinct

A morning's stretch paves a way for the new
Still I can't be without you

A field filled with nothing but space must appear
to be the most emptiest
But that is not true, for I am the most emptiest
without you

When the sun sets and dawn turns to dusk
I always think about you
When my eyes open and my eyes shut
I will always think about you

So beautiful, so pure and so distinct.

Lush
"Sundae Lush"

This rosy pink that I wear on the arch of my
cheeks
doesn't come from the bitter cold
but from the intense conversations you and I
forever hold...
Sweeter than pure sugar stuck at the bottom of
my cold drink
With you, I never over-think
Drunk in love, every day I over drink...
I'm a Sundae Lush!
I want to indulge in all of your flavors
The good, the bad, the ugly
I wouldn't change a thing, I love how ya mommy
made ya...
We took it from minor to major,
but we're the only two players.
God answered my prayers when I asked for
something sweet...
He sent me overflowing layers of trust, honesty
and commitment...

A solid foundation and some of my favorite
toppings: Romance, Chemistry and a whole lot of
Communication.
He sprinkled on a little bit of attitude, and the part
I love the most,
was the part that sank to the bottom, a kind
heart...my cherry on top!
So when they ask why I wear this rosy pink on the
arch of my cheeks,
I swear I tell em' it's 'cause I'm his cherry on top.

Lush
"What a Handful"

On egg shells he never walks
A good game he often talks
Attitude pretty nonchalant
And the fact that I love him is the hardest part

On the wrong side of the bed he wakes
Risky chances he loves to take
Mistakes and "uh o's" he often makes
A love far from perfect but even further from fake

Bad days, worse nights
Name calling and petty fights
What can I say we're a couple, this is what we do
and we do it well
Everything is fine, dandy and going super swell
Kidding, I'm a terrible liar, so the truth you could
easily tell

Insecurity and jealousy shouldn't take place
but it does and when it hits it's written all over the
face
He say and she say that he ain't this
but all we do is smile at the good times that are
filled with bliss

For we love our haters and congratulators all the same.

You couldn't tell us nada about each other that we knew not of
Plenty pet peeves, and flaws
Granny draws and messy floors
Yucky food and monstrous snores
The fluffy marshmallow that completes his chocolate smore
I'm all of that and so much more
Two hands aren't enough for this guy
I swear I ask myself "what did I get myself into?"
Time after time
Only the heart knows.

Lush
"Circle the Block"

I circle the block, I circle the block, I circle the
block
Because parking around here
really...fucking...sucks
So I circle the block, I circle the block, I circle the
block, I circle.
Searching for a deeper space, a different space, a
space with more depth.

I'm running out of gas, losing my breath
Sweating out this perm
Wearing a long face of concern
Right, left, I'm unsure of which way to turn
All I hear is horns and a swarm of bad words that
our mothers taught us never to repeat
So I make a left, hastily
And just my luck I end up at a dead end, are you
fucking kidding me?!
Jammed pack, busted windows
Garbage and road kill, the stench seeps through
my window, I'm almost ready to puke!

I broke the fastest broken u-turn that you'd ever see, speeding to make it back to safety!

So again I circle the block, I circle the block, I circle the block
Because parking around here
really...fucking...sucks
So I circle the block, I circle the block, I circle the block, I circle.
Searching for a deeper space, a different space, a space with more depth.

And I circle the block, I circle the block, I circle the block
Because parking around here
really...fucking...sucks
So I circle the block, I circle the block, I circle the block, I circle.
I cannot seem to find a deeper person, a different person, a person with more depth.
A person whom is worth the struggle of making myself fit within them
Inching to get into their mind, to their heart, to their soul...

Becoming one with one another
All of these spaces are just a waste of space to
me!

So I circle the block, I circle the block, I circle the
block
Because parking around here
really...fucking...sucks!
And I am just so, so tired of searching for the right
space.
For the right person, for a deeper person, for a
person with more depth.

No matter how tiresome I might grow
I will not settle for just any john doe
Knowing your self-worth is so important,
And I won't hesitate to let any and everyone
know.

Lush
"When the Summer Ends"

He was like a long snooze after a road trip gone
terribly wrong
Like a ray of sunshine after a frightening storm
He was like a catchy hook to a tacky love song
Like a blow to some food that was way too warm

We spoke and touched with our eyes
I watched him watch me, he watched me watch
him
It was like I was his reflection and he was mine
Like somehow we came together and combined

The time we shared was simply magic
We danced, we laughed, and we loved
Shared stories from our past, some epic, some
tragic
We kissed, we argued, even shoved

The summer came to an end, and I had to watch
him ride off in his father's mini van
It felt like as if my heart got ripped out of my chest

I felt my breath escape from my lungs, entirely,
there was nothing left
I couldn't speak; all I could do was grab at the air,
wishing it was him
Oh how I wish it was him, I wish it were his face,
for one last kiss
A kiss that would be endless

You see, he was my first love
and I knew that I'd love him for a lifetime
The first time that we caught each other's eyes,
never wanting to look away, to look no further
There was no need; he was all I ever wanted
I'd wish upon a wishing well
For my true love to hurry back

He was only a couple of hundred miles away
His dad packed up the family with promises that
they'd shortly return
They changed phone numbers frequently,
so a pen pal I became
I swear if I had enough money in my piggy bank,
I'd fly to see him

If I were old enough to drive, I'd race to his place
If I were even allowed to stay out past nine!
Maybe then everything would be remotely fine

The summer is back around and what a long
winter it was
The wait was sooo unbearable
I begged my mom to push my curfew to ten, as I
was a year older then
She smiled and said "since you did such a good job
in school make it 10:30"
For joy I jumped, I cheesed all through the night
Blake was a little older and his parents were more
lenient, so he hadn't any worries,
we hadn't any worries
Except for when the summer ended

We longed to feel the summer wind!
But hated to see the summer end
We hated to see the summer win
But longed to see the summer begin!

Lush
 "Don't shoot me down"

I don't want to be another pretty face in your past
I don't want to be another girl that you just
bang, bang, bang
Shoot!
Please don't shoot me down
You clipped my wings and I landed on your
doorsteps; this unfamiliar ground
I don't think I know what really just hit me
I think I'm afraid to find out.

I don't want to be another pretty face in your past
I don't want to be another girl that you just
bang, bang, bang
Shoot!
I've fallen! I've fallen! Can't seem to get up
You took my heart in your hand and as soon as
you grew bored
You put it down, never returning it to its rightful
place
You should be ashamed, but you're not
Hasn't your mother ever taught you to put things
back where they belong?

I don't want to be another pretty face in your past
I don't want to be another girl that you just
bang, bang, bang
Shoot!
Please don't shoot me down

Why aim and fire
When I'm not what your heart desires
You turned on my flames, just to put them out
Stomp them out
Wet me up, pat me down
I begged you not to shoot me down
Now I'm wounded, afraid to leave ground
My wings won't flap, my heart skips beat
My rhythms are totally off
All I ever wanted to do ...was fly
For I knew, if I ever were to run into someone like
you
That I'd just become
Another pretty face in your past, another girl that
you'd just bang, bang, bang shoot!

Stop! Don't shoot
Whatever you do
Please don't shoot me down!

Lush
"A Tribute to Love"- (Myia & John)

It was a day like any other day in the hot month
of June
Never would I have thought it be the day that
changed my life forever
Everything happened so fast, so soon
We became familiar with each other, some would
even say smother
Every day, every minute we wanted to be near
All the love and the pain all we wanted to do was
share
Filled with car rides, drinks, laughs and a whole
bunch of tears
Can't forget that Rose gang music, good music for
your ears!
Ups, downs got my head spinning all around
My heart's jumping out of my chest
Wish I could fast forward just to see what's gonna
happen next
Because I dreamt it would be perfect...
But who wants that perfect love story anyway
Cliché', cliché'!

I'd fast forward just to rewind and re-live every
moment with you
The good, the bad and the ugly, for you I'd take it
all
For you I'd risk it all
Some ask why I'm still here,
riding like a trooper
I tell em' I'm taking a shot at love, I'm a Hooper
Things get shaky at times but freak it I'm a hoper
There are only a few things I'm addicted to,
and one of them is you
The other is café (Coffee) no *Europa'*
Oh and my nails and hair, no need to continue
I only have eyes for you, no need to browse the
menu
I'm not looking, I'm taken! I tell em' with pride
Shut em' down if they try.

You know I miss you; it's so hard to sleep
There have been issues before
but this one's so deep
It takes the cake, yup the biggest piece
You're always in my heart, on my mind, never will
it cease

Keep your head up, *"my pride and joy baby boy*
I love you to death, till my last breath!"
They say it gets better in time
So only time will tell...
Through it all I'm still in love with you,
and I'm so happy that I fell!

Prince Isaac
"A Force" Inspired by Love

I am in awe when I'm struck with a thought of you
I make the futile attempt to find the appropriate
comparison, yet despite how vast this planet is
I am unable to detect a match in regard of how
you make me feel.
Indeed there are many beautiful sights upon earth
however, none can measure to yours,
that is your external and internal beauty.

With this projection of you on my mental screen
I am often left with feeling overwhelming
pensiveness, for to be disenfranchised of you
on the physical plane is torturous to the soul!
I enter the theatre as a child entering a candy
store without being permitted to have at least one
bite of any candy, very much petulant and
saddened, alas my beloved, this is how I am!

But I am able to maintain equilibrium, for I know
in due time I will be able to indulge in your beauty
daily.

My heart flutters when I think about being able to awake to that radiant smile, a smile that can easily upset the sun, by replacing it as the light of earth. Upon you entering this gloomy abode instantly it's illuminated, and I am immediately energized with zeal that only you can produce.

Oh I wish I could use such energy to fly from here to you, even if it's for a mere moment, I yearn just to wrap my arms around you.
Your body fits so perfectly in between my arms, as if you were molded just for me.
The softness of your body is how one would imagine a cloud. In your embrace I find solace...
In your kiss I find fire and desire...
In your eyes I see the force that has mystified man for ages, a force that is more powerful than any bomb, more beautiful than any wonder of the world. A force that will keep us bound in an orbit of our own, that force my beloved is a force that I possess regarding you, a force I shall never relinquish, a force I will use to compel me to bring you nothing less than bliss.
That force my dearest, is Love!

Lush
"Prince Charming"

We came from two different worlds
He was unknown to me, like a foreign creature
I think his mind was his best feature
See I fell in love with the way he thought
Then I fell in love with his voice, how it assured
certainty
And certainly but not last, I fell in love with his
heart, overlooked his past
Many miles apart we may be
But when it comes to this love connection
There's no ifs, ands, buts nor maybes

I think I stole his heart with my unique and silly
laugh, (giggles)
Which he makes me do so often
He makes me whole, like two ends on a freshly
baked loaf
He holds me together, so I'll never have to
experience being broken
Crumbled, disarrayed
He's my Prince Charming, it's true

No fairy tales, no glass slippers
I was a damsel in distress
and he rescued me from this cruel and lonely
world
He is my Prince Charming, yes it's true

We were made for each other
Made to be strong....willing, ready and able
We received each other
Made love to each other; using just words
And oh how we use our words so superbly
that we create such a vivid picture
We are visionaries! To say the least
He's a movement by himself, but together we are
a beast
What's mine is his, and what's his is mine so
together we will eat
and that's all the time
He's on my mind...all the time, wouldn't shake
him out if I could
If I could kiss him every second of the minute,
then I would
He is my Prince Charming, it's true

With my eyes closed, and my hands tied; with all
senses gone
He's truly sublime, and I'd pick him every time
For he is my Prince Charming, oh yes it's true!

Lush
"The Thought of You"

Most days I'm empty
So much so, that tears race down my cheeks
Sometimes I'm happy
But just enough to get through the day
It can be hard and long

Most days I find myself stuck on the thought of
you
So much so, that everything and one around me,
becomes inadmissible
Sometimes I'm focused
But just enough to get through the day
It is so hard, and so long

I cry sometimes; when it's just me in the room
And it's just me in the room most of the time
I find myself completely alone
Completely incomplete
I dream a lot, of you I dream of
I love it when I dream of you, when I think it's
real, when I think it's true

Most days I'm empty
Except for the nights that I dream of you
So real and so true
I am utterly complete
Stuck in the thought

I am utterly complete when I am stuck in the thought of you.

Lush
"Gentle & Understanding"

Too many times I have been placed with "the bad
guy," when you came into my life I figured that
would be over, the last of it
And though the judicial system labeled you with
that title, my heart didn't,
my heart couldn't
My spirit felt right with you
It danced and it sung, and it moved in ways it
hadn't moved in years
My first love made me feel a similar soppiness
I imagined this would be how my final and eternal
love would make me feel...

Too many times I've heard "you are just too good
of a person to be treated like this"
When you came into my life I figured that would
be over, the last of it,
the last time I'd hear those words
Instead they would speak words like: you two are
perfect for each other, girl after all those frogs
you've experienced... you finally found your
prince.
and I'm hoping that's so true
not because I'm desperate, but because I don't
know how much more my heart can take

How many more times my heart can be
reassembled and re-stitched...
after all of the torment from the innumerable
blows and kicks...

After every following encounter, the skin only gets
thicker
And the patience runs lower, and tolerance gets
shorter
real short, like I don't mean to take it out on you
but this is unacceptable, short
to make a long story short...
your love should be kind, and gentle, and genuine
and understanding
I promise to always make sure mine reflects those
very words
And if ever they don't, please let me know
You told me if you were ever to make any errors
to immediately inform you
and you'd correct them...

So my love, my final and eternal love...
I ask you not to make my heart anymore tattered
But to keep it warm, sheltered and whole
For in the end, happiness and love were all that
mattered.

Lush
"If I Miss Your Call"

I'm afraid to close my eyes for even a brief
moment
Afraid to even throw my phone on the charger for
some juice
Boy, if I miss your call

If I miss your call I think I'd go insane
The absence of your voice,
so sultry and seductive
I think I'd lose my mind, at the absence of your
voice

I'd tuck my phone between my bra strap and
breast, apprehensive about being too far,
unable to run to my phone
To hear that voice, and the words that they utter
Compliments, tasks, more compliments and how
was your day?
Boy, if I miss your call

Oh if I miss your call I think I'd go insane
I know I'd be off
My day would be filled with mayhem

My thoughts would be cluttered
and my words would be stuttered
At the absence of your voice,
so sultry and seductive
I think I'd lose my mind, at the absence of your
voice

If I miss your call
Knowing I couldn't dial your number back

I wait for your call everyday
I long for your call in everyway
I need to hear your voice, right now
and every now that there will be...
If I miss your call.

Lush
"A Prison Love Story"

I want to start writing about our story
This will be like a journal entry for our story is still
being written...

I want to discover all of your flaws and all of your
strengths
I want you to discover mine
Explore me baby, and please take your time
I want to go through the stages
You know, instantly replying to your messages,
filled with kissy faces and hearts
Sleep with my phone next to my pillow,
Cause' I can't miss not one of your calls
I want to dream about us, just drifting away
I picture just me and you
Making love in all types of ways
I want to tell you I love you, so I do
And you tell me you love me too,
In fact, more

I want this story... our story,
to be everything we imagine it to be
You said you never thought that you could fall
in love
Damn baby, that's make me feel so special
Like I'm so one of a kind
Your number one lady
I can't help but blush
With just a wink of your eye
and a lick of your lips
I'm yours
And all yours

Our love story is indeed odd, but so true
A bit strange, but so right
We fell in love at a time drenched in adversity
And it was least expected
And that my love is the best part of our story

Our Prison Love Story...

Prince Isaac
"Beauty"

Beauty is in the eye of the beholder, so I'm told
This woman I find beautiful, wasn't based on
physical appearance alone.
My initial contact with her was via phone.
In a course of several conversations affinity
blossomed like a rosebud in spring.
Her qualities and character make her a superb
being.

When my eyes came to see this beautiful Lady,
I couldn't believe God released one of his angels
to me.
Like the sunset on a vast sea, this beautiful Lady
reflected beauty ideally to me.
Her smile was bright, and white as snow
Far more supreme than any portrait by Michael
Angelo.
Her eyes enchanting and hypnotizing, staring into
them I felt like I was rising into the air,
while they conveyed I have nothing to fear.

I feel nothing but glee, thinking how this beautiful
Lady is solely for me, I frequently daydream of the
day I swim her sea.
The visual is clear, me between her knee,
propelling her body into soaring heights of
ecstasy.
I swim deep, as far as I can, expertly navigating
her waters like no other man.

Indeed, this beautiful Lady has taken a hold of me.
One day I will drop to a knee, ask her to be my
wife.
So I can spend the rest of my life with this
beauteous being.

LUSH
"GIVE LOVE A FIGHTING CHANCE"

I LOVE RECEIVING SWEET SCRIBES FROM MY
GUY...
HIS CHOICE OF WORDS, SO WHOLE-HEARTED
AND BONA FIDE...
I FALL INTO A HIGH, SURPASSING THE CLOUDS
IN THE SKY...
IT'S AN ABSLOUTE OH MY! KIND OF FEELING
THAT I CANNOT HIDE...

HE POSSESSES ALL OF THE QUALITIES THAT A
WOMAN SEARCHES FOR...
BRAVENESS, ENDURANCE, HUMORITY AND
MOST OF ALL A WARM HEART...
TO ME HE IS EVERY THING, THE ONLY THING
AND SO MUCH MORE...
IF DISTANCE HAD NO EXISTENCE WE WOULD
NEVER BE APART...

I'M INTO HIM, LIKE HE'S INTO ME, AND THAT'S
WHEN YOU KNOW IT'S REAL...
HE LOVES MY HEART, MIND AND SOUL, MY
LAUGH HAD HIM SOLD...

NEITHER WORDS NOR EXPRESSIONS CAN
DESCRIBE HOW HE MAKES ME FEEL...
I AM ON TOP OF THE WORLD, IN HIS EYES, IN
HIS KISS, IN HIS HOLD...

THOUGH IN THE PAST I HAVE BEEN
CONTINUOSLY LET DOWN...
I WILL GIVE THIS GREAT MAN A FIGHTING
CHANCE...
HE HAS PROVEN WORTHY TO BE KING, ON HIS
HEAD I AM ELATED TO PLACE THEE CROWN...
OUR LOVE IS A TYPE OF LOVE YOU CAN SEE
FROM FIRST GLANCE...
WE'D BE THE BIGGEST FOOLS TO NOT GIVE
LOVE A FIGHTING CHANCE.

Lush
"Rocking Me"

I feel the chills at my shoulders
with a mere thought of you
I feel the tears, those of joy
I feel them roll down my face
with a mere thought of the way you love me, the
way you hypnotize me
Rocking me...

Ooh your love rocks me
into a heavenly sleep, I'm at peace
We dance in my dreams
to a few of our favorite love songs
And sometimes, just to the rhythm of our heart
beats
Our lips sing along
And our tongues chime in
We create everlasting ad-libs from sweet and
intensifying moans
They grow and they grow
Don't stop
Rocking me...

Ooh your love rocks me...

There's never a bumpy ride with you by my side
But I know for certain, if there were ever
We'd be strapped in
Ready for whatever
Ahoy captain!
'Cause with you I could take on the world
With just your love
Rocking me in swirls
Rocking me...

Ooh how your love rocks me.

Lush
"I Love You Because"

I'll love you from the lowest valley
From the highest mountain
And the longest river
I'll love you because...

I'll love you after you make me angry
From the smallest of things
And even the biggest ones too
I'll love you because...

I'll love you while you're facing adversity
While they try to keep a good man down
While they try to make you lose
I'll forever be around to help you win
I'll love you because...

I love you because you'll always fight
(When it's important)
I love you because you're not always right
(Because you're human)

I love you because...
When my eyes lay upon a picture of you
I can't help but to kiss it
And when I'm disenfranchised from toughing you,
oh how much do I miss it
(Because it hurts)
I love you because...
Well, I love you because you're you.

Lush
"Live There"

I want to lie on your chest
and stay there, live there
I want to learn your heart's rhythm
and record it, only to discover that it matches
mine
I want to just be near you
I want to bug you and annoy you
Kiss you and adore you
Stare at you while you sleep
and complain about the gritting of your teeth
I want you to play with my hair as I sleep,
and I'd deny that I snore, even though you have
me on tape
I want to experience it all,
and only with you
Giving you as much of me, that you can take...

You fell upon me
But you'd say it was the other way around
but lord knows I asked for you

and God only grants you what you need not what
you want
Though of course I want you too.
Love me? Of course I'm glad you do
and I promise to be the best woman for you, and
to you
Every day I know you strive to be the best for
me...you're almost perfect
and we all know almost doesn't count
but in my eyes you'll always be the 'bestest'

Ooo visions and thoughts of you
make my stomach twirl and my heart do flips
Overflowing emotions, for I am an emotional
rollercoaster
but your love keeps me on kilter
You show me your true colors
no make-up, no filter
It is sublime love in the air...
I inhale it as if I need it to live,
to keep my heart pumping
Some men run away from love
but you my king, embrace it,
understand it and face it...happily

So you place my head on your chest
and I stay there, and I live there
'cause without words you ask me to,
and without asking I'd gladly do.

Lush
"When I Met You"

If I had met you under different circumstances
I think maybe I'd give you a chance, even chances
Your stance, your stare, it pulls me in
But I am strong
Lust will not win...I tell myself constantly

If I had met you maybe a year ago
I think maybe I would have given you a chance
A glance, your stare, it pulls me in
But I am strong
Lust will not win...I tell myself constantly

You caught me at a wrong time,
 I surely wasn't prepared
You kissed me at a wrong time,
your lips I couldn't compare...the feel,
the way that they pressed against mine, so divine
I wanted to walk away, pull away, distance myself
But I was so weak
Lust wanted to win, and it did...she won

Maybe if you had loved me a little less
I think possibly I could've walked away
Your hold, your stare, it pulled me in
It kept me in, in your arms, under your spell
And I wasn't going anywhere, ever
Lust was now love, sweet and kind
And it was all because I gave you a chance
At that exact moment, which I thought was wrong
All wrong, but it was all right

When I met you...

Lush
"Most Incredible Feeling"

In his hands lie my insecurities
In his hands lie my despair, my doubts
For he has removed that from me

In his actions I find strength
In his actions I find tenacity, hope
For he has instilled that in me

And I've never gotten that from any other man
Instead it was fear, anger
All they ever did was try to belittle me
To lower my self-assurance
I would be in denial if I said it didn't work for
awhile
But that awhile was very short-lived
And today I am stronger than I've ever been
More loved than I've ever been...
It is the single most incredible feeling that
I've ever experienced.

No, everyday isn't a sunny day
and every night isn't spent making passionate love
but it is one that is spent together
It is one that is true...that is take me as I am
Love all of me, or none of me at all
And we do...
and it is the single most incredible feeling that I've
ever experienced.

Lush
"Will you still?"

I want you to still be here when the rain clears
(Waking up to your face)
Will you still love me when my hair thins, will you?
'cause I'll still love you, with everything I've got...

I want you to still be the reason for my smiles
(and boy do I smile a lot)
Will you still be that one that drives me wild?
'cause I'll always be around, giving everything I've
got...

See my love won't stop
and my love won't quit
So I'm praying and asking that yours won't forfeit
'cause you're everything I've wanted, and
everything I need

Will you, will you...
Tell me I'm your favorite girl
The number one lady in your world
I can't even describe, the way you make me feel
inside

'cause I'm gon' love you for life
So baby please tell me...
Will you still be there when the rain clears?
Will you still love me when my hair thins?
'cause I'll still love you, with everything I've got...
Giving everything I've got.

~~Only

For The

Grown And Sexy~~

~~~~~~~~~~~~~~~~~~~~~~~~~~~~~~~~~~~~~

Lush
"This Impact"

Slower, slower go even slower
Even lower
Don't rush this impact
The nibble of the nipple
Makes my heart beat triple, tremble

Faster, faster go even faster
Even nastier
But don't rush this impact
The suck of the head
Makes his heart beat triple, tremble

His hands dance down by my waist
He tastes me, in a minute's time my sweet fluids
trickle down his face

Slow, fast, slow, fast...don't forget the circles
Even deeper
But don't rush this impact
This impact, this impact, this impact!
Oooh the climax lays me flat on my back

Another round! He yells
Another round!

Lush
"The Number Game"

It's been **10** days and **9** long nights since our
bodies touched
While you were gone I dreamt of your body's
touch
I reminisced of the way your mouth French
kissed my...**EVERTHING!!**
In and out, out and in you'd maneuver that
elongated tongue.

I let out **8** moans and **7** screams of pure ecstasy
I kept count for you were the only one that took
me to that mount...
To the top of the moon and back,
and it all started from a little spooning from the
back.

You pushed my head down **6** times and **5**
minutes later you shook like an earthquake,
erupted like a volcano
I slurped and swished it all around,
as you held firmly to my brown ass (so bouncy
and so round).

We took **4** shots of Patron and **3** gulps of tequila
You squirted lemon and salted my navel
Slowly you sucked it clean and dry
and although I squirmed, you proceeded to drip
hot wax all down my spleen, **Iye Papi!!**
I screamed "don't be so mean!" (But please don't
be too kind).

That night our **2** bodies became **1**, and we had **0**
restrictions
We did tricks, flips, dips and all types of
acrobatic shit
That night we turned up and turned out!

Lush
"Black Horse"

Well for starters, the man was...
well-endowed, I mean he was extremely talented
He taught me tricks that only a new dog would
try
Tricks that only an old dog could master
He demanded that he's to call me master!
He did any and everything I wanted
Although his imagination exceeded mine,
I kept up!
If the big black horse went down
I got him up! Right back...

His muscular arms held me captive
(Not like I wanted to escape)
We played dress up, I was his Lois...
He wore the cape...
And only the cape
Like an ape, he'd beat his chest
He was an animal
The dirtiest of them all
But boy was he well-endowed
He was freaking hung!

Easy! Take it easy baby
You know you can't just ram that big ole thing
in lil ole me
Oh but you like this strain on my face huh?!
The tears that I cry
When I reach my hands behind me to push you
back, I think you like that
Showing your strength
You naughty boy!

Black horse, my black horse
That's what I told my girls his name was.
Magnificent, the pipe game was
From start to finish
He wiggled in the middle
But his back was strong
And his tongue was long
Oh my! And was it wide
Ladies did I mention, he was freaking huunngg!
Like a horse
Like a black horse.

Lush
"Sex in the Window"

Let's have sex in the window by the roses
(Sex in the window by the pink roses)
We don't even gotta move them
Neighbors are watching, we'll just moon them
'Cause we ain't got nothing to hide
So baby let's have sex in the window

I don't wanna get up off this window seal
Baby you know it's feeling way too surreal
My body, I won't conceal
Miniature kisses all up and down my spine
Your lips, so juicy and divine

Baby let's go slower
Let's not rush this moment
Baby let's go deeper
Let's just make it last forever
Or at least until the sun goes down

Let's have sweet sex in the window by the roses
(Sex in the window by the pink roses)
We don't even gotta move them
Neighbors are watching, we'll just moon them
'Cause we ain't got nothing to hide
So baby let's... have sex... in the window.

Lush
"Anticipation"

I can't wait til that day comes…
the day when we can make sweet and passionate
love
when we can fuck, and be animals in the wild
I just want to be wrapped in those arms
Even just for awhile…sitting in your lap, with
my legs around your waist
while my body lies against yours
and my lips won't stop attacking your face
they'll lose control, but you'll like it… and I'll
love it
there'd be no other place I'd want to be

I wait patiently for that most anticipated day
When it comes there will be neither interruptions
nor malfunctions
Just introductions and productions
My body meets your body
We'll unwind and intertwine
Shedding all insecurities
Exposing each other's goodies
You'll knock and I'll pull you in
Taking all of you in, slowly but entirely

We'd tire each other out,
but once rejuvenated the magic happens all over
again

Right now we craft love scenes and paint
pictures
But soon enough we'll be able to do that with
more than just our minds
And it will be the best...
and absolutely divine!

Lush
"Exploration"

Wrapped in a silk robe
Purple as a plum
He just stared at me and hummed

Sweet lady of mine,
come here and show me what I've been missing, he
said to me
With lips so plump and juicy

"With those deep eyes, tell me what you see
when looking at me?"
Beauty…in its rarest of forms
I see sunlight in your smile, very much warm
Pizzazz in your strut
Love in your heart
And a big ole bubble butt

(Giggles) We both laugh
And with my glass of Moscato wine I make my
way over to you
Pushing you on the bed with my free hand
As you tumble back I hop aboard
"I want to ride you, am I tall enough?"

Without words you spoke back to me
Flipping me over on my back, showing me who's
in charge
My clear wine wets the bed but we play in it
instead
I told you I can get wetter
And I always keep my word...

Disrobed, as you attempted to remove my
panties you noticed I wore none
Your eyes, damn those pretty eyes, they grew
wider
Filled with excitement
Every inch of my body you explored
Not one area ignored

How I love it when you take your time
How I love it when you blow my mind
Bend my spine and slaughter it from behind
It should be consider a crime...
I'm left stumped, entire body numb
And you- so amused at what great job you've
done

Once my body regains mobility
I'll show him things he's never experienced
I'll get the last laugh...I promise. *Wink*

www.ingramcontent.com/pod-product-compliance
Lightning Source LLC
Chambersburg PA
CBHW021131020426
42331CB00005B/712